ANCIENT NUMBERS!

The Math of **Counting Systems**

Written by Anne Rooney

www.worldbook.com

Co-published by agreement between Shi Tu Hui and World Book, Inc.

Shi Tu Hui
Room 1807, Block 1,
#3 West Dawang Road
Chaoyang District, Beijing 100025
P.R. China

World Book, Inc.
180 North LaSalle Street
Suite 900
Chicago, Illinois 60601
USA

© 2026. All rights reserved. This volume may not be reproduced in whole or in part in any form without prior written permission from the publisher.

WORLD BOOK and the GLOBE DEVICE are registered trademarks or trademarks of World Book, Inc.

Library of Congress Control Number: 2025942097

Aha! Academy: Math
ISBN: 978-0-7166-7377-4 (set, hardcover)

Ancient Numbers! The Math of Counting Systems
ISBN: 978-0-7166-7378-1 (hard cover)
ISBN: 978-0-7166-7441-2 (e-book)
ISBN: 978-0-7166-7431-3 (soft cover)

Staff

Editorial

Vice President
Tom Evans

Editorial Project Coordinator
Kaile Kilner

Senior Curriculum Designer
Caroline Davidson

Curriculum Designer
Mikayla Kightlinger

Proofreader
Nathalie Strassheim

Indexer
Nathaniel Lindstrom

Graphics and Design

Senior Visual
Communications Designer
Melanie Bender

Designer
Shannon Hagman

Written by Anne Rooney

Designed by Starletta Polster

Acknowledgments

The publishers gratefully acknowledge the following sources for photography. All illustrations were prepared by WORLD BOOK unless otherwise noted.

Cover: Nomad Pixel/Shutterstock; PhotoSongserm/Shutterstock; Redshinestudio/Shutterstock; Viacheslav Lopatin/Shutterstock; yevgeniy11/Shutterstock

© The History Collection/Alamy 11; © MET/BOT/Alamy 13; © Science History Images/Alamy; ESO/Landessternwarte Heidelberg-Königstuhl/F. W. Dyson, A. S. Eddington, & C. Davidson (licensed under CC BY 4.0) 41; Josell7 (licensed under CC BY-SA 4.0) 12; Marie-Lan Nguyen (licensed under CC BY 2.5) 11; NASA 42; Public Domain 19, 23, 24; © Shutterstock 4, 5, 6, 7, 8, 9, 10, 11, 12, 13, 14, 15, 16, 17, 18, 19, 20, 21, 22, 23, 24, 25, 26, 27, 28, 29, 30, 31, 32, 33, 34, 35, 36, 37, 38, 39, 40, 41, 42, 43, 44, 45, 46, 47, 48; Winchester City Council Museums (licensed under CC BY-SA 2.0) 9

There is a glossary of terms on page 48. Terms defined in the glossary are in type that looks like *this* on their first appearance on any spread (two facing pages).

Contents

Introduction 4
① **Learning to count** 6
   Tools for tallying 8
   Counting in clay 10
   1, 2, 3 ... start writing! 12
   Making measurements 14
② **A number of numbers** 16
   Write like a Roman 18
   Chinese numbers 20
   From India to Baghdad 22
   New numbers for a new age 24
③ **Get in position** 26
   Put in your place! 28
   Zero, the hero 30
   Less than zero 32
④ **Number bases** 34
   Count on your fingers 36
   Dozens of eggs? .38
   60 minutes in an hour 40
   Alien numbers 42
Make your own number system! 44
Index 46
Glossary 48

Introduction

We use numbers every day, but have you thought about where they come from? Or why they look the way they do? With numbers, we can count, tell the time and date, show prices, measure and weigh things (including ourselves), keep score in games and sport—and do math.

Measuring your feet makes sure your new shoes fit.

People have used numbers for thousands of years. The squiggly shapes we now use as numbers have changed over that time. Even how we think of numbers relating to each other has changed. People have always made large numbers from strings of symbols, but they have done it in different ways.

We couldn't live in the modern world without numbers. Read on to see how people have used numbers in the past and in different parts of the world, and find out how we got the numbers we use now.

We used 2,300,000 blocks of stone.

1 LEARNING TO COUNT

We didn't develop any written numbers until about 5,000 years ago. Some time before that we must have come up with numbers for counting, but before even that people first kept track of quantities by tallying. This is registering objects or events without actually counting them, using a mark, a pebble, or another object to correspond to each item.

You probably learned to count before you started school, and count now without even thinking about it. But there was a time before human beings counted.

Not only humans have an idea of number; some birds can tell if one of their eggs or chicks is missing.

A tally can be a line of strokes.

Not everyone counts—not everyone needs to. Living deep in the Amazon jungle, the Pirahã people have no words for colors or numbers, and don't work with groups of more than three items. Their way of life does not need numbers.

Counting is more useful than tallying. It gives us a way of talking about quantities and working with them—the start of math! Read on to find out how humans first began to use numbers and learn to count.

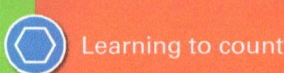 Learning to count

Tools for **tallying**

The first morning, you collect some pebbles. As each goat leaves their pen, you move a pebble. When all 20 goats have left, you will have 20 pebbles piled together—even though you don't know it's 20.

In the evening, you move a pebble for each goat as it comes in. If there are pebbles left over, you need to go and look for the lost goats. If you have moved all the pebbles, all your goats are safe.

TECH TIME

Have you seen a steward clicking a hand-held clicker to tally people going into a music festival or sports venue? This little electronic device registers each click as an item to count. The click-counter does the counting—the user is tallying, just like a Stone Age shepherd!

Click! Click!

Imagine you have 20 goats, but you can't count. Every evening, you must check that all your goats are safely shut away from wolves. You can do this by tallying.

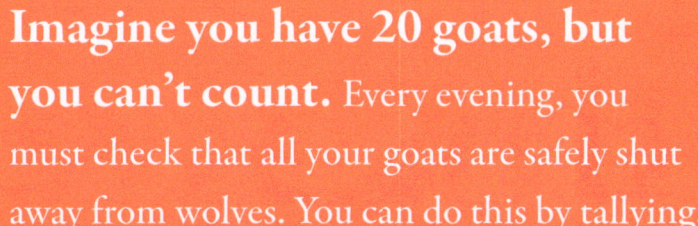

A common way to tally is to make four marks, then strike through the group to make five.

The oldest surviving mathematical object is a baboon's leg bone carved with 29 notches 40,000 years ago in what is now Eswatini. We don't know what the notches on this tallying stick represent—perhaps days of the moon's cycle, or someone's goats.

If you've ever played a game where you make a mark for each turn, or if you have kept a count (perhaps of passing cars, or birds in your garden), you've used tallying.

The English tax system used tally sticks from the 1100's to 1826. The width of a cut showed its value. In 1834, sticks stored over hundreds of years were burned—starting a fire that destroyed the English Parliament building.

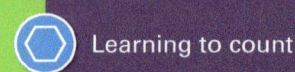
Learning to count

Counting in clay

Over 8,000 years ago, people in the area around Syria began making clay tokens to stand for possessions, such as sheep, goats, or grain. If you had one sheep, you had one token. For two sheep, you had two tokens.

To avoid using too many tokens, people added larger tokens for groups of 10 or 60 items. They used different shapes for different objects. These tokens might count as the first "written" numbers: a cone meant "1" and a sphere meant "10."

Counting is much more useful than tallying.
But written numbers didn't come straight from tallying.

Having all those tokens lying around must have been inconvenient. About 5,500 years ago, people began to seal their tokens inside a clay ball called a "bulla." They could trade the sealed ball as it stood for the things they owned. Any argument about what someone owned could be settled by smashing the ball and counting the tokens.

People pressed a picture of the tokens into the clay ball so that they didn't need to keep breaking them. Finally, the ball and tokens gave way to just marks on the clay—flat clay tablets recorded what people owned, owed, or traded.

Learning to count

1, 2, 3 ... start writing!

The oldest numbers grew out of tallying. If you wanted to show "9," you drew nine lines. It would get tricky if you kept on going like that, so people drew a new symbol to stand for "10." They used that up to five times in a row. It still took up a lot of space, taking 14 marks to represent 59 (nine "1" marks and five "10" marks).

1	11	21	31	41	51
2	12	22	32	42	52
3	13	23	33	43	53
4	14	24	34	44	54
5	15	25	35	45	55
6	16	26	36	46	56
7	17	27	37	47	57
8	18	28	38	48	58
9	19	29	39	49	59
10	20	30	40	50	

The Sumerians invented this system more than 5,000 years ago (3300 B.C.) in Mesopotamia. They pressed their number symbols into wet clay with a wedge-shaped stick, making spiky, angular marks. Their script is called cuneiform and it was later used for writing words, too. The same system was used by the Babylonians who lived in the area later.

The very first things people wrote weren't words, but numbers—math clearly mattered to our ancestors!

The ancient Egyptians also repeated symbols to build up numbers.

1	/	A tally mark
10	∩	A cattle hobble
100	℮	A coil of rope
1,000	⚲	A lotus flower
10,000	𓂭	A bent finger
100,000	𓆏	A tadpole
1,000,000	𓁨	Heh, a figure who represented infinity

= 10,426

In early cities, people wanted to record what they owned, their taxes, and plots of land. Math was just what they needed! They soon found they could use it to track the movements of planets and stars, starting the science of astronomy.

A scribe wrote cuneiform by pressing a stylus (shaped stick) into soft clay. The clay hardened as it dried.

Count my toes!

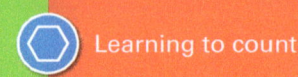
Learning to count

Making measurements

At first, people used parts of their own bodies to measure. We still use a "foot" as a unit of measure. People have also used the distance from elbow to fingertip (a "cubit"), a hand span, or a thumb's width (an inch).

People are different sizes, though. It's no good if one person's foot is 12 inches and another is 11 inches! Measures had to be standardized to be truly useful. So the king's foot or cubit became the standard measure, and people began to use rods of that length for measuring.

People needed to measure weight and volume to trade fairly. Dry goods like grain were first measured by volume—in a hollow gourd, for example.

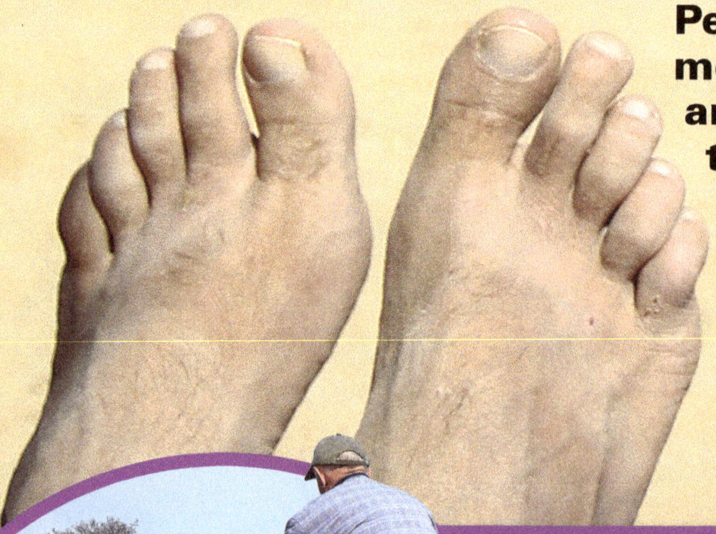

You can measure while moving, too. Distances could be measured in paces. An area of land could be defined by how long it took to mow or plough.

You can't build a pyramid if everyone is using different sized blocks of stone!
People needed consistent measurements to build, record ownership of land, and plan journeys.

The ancient Egyptians used math to plan and build their buildings, monuments, and pyramids.

Some types of grain and seed are very regular sizes and weights. The "carat" was originally a carob seed. It's still used as a weight measurement for gems and gold.

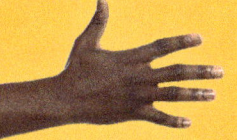

Ancient Greeks used the width of a finger (daktylos) as a measure. A knuckle was 2 fingers, a palm was 4 fingers and a full hand span was 12 fingers.

Whose feet are a foot?

DID YOU KNOW?

There are special units for measuring lots of odd things. There is a scale for how hot chilies are (measured in Scoville Heat Units, or SHU), how much space sickness an astronaut suffers (measured in Garns), and the quality of soil based on how many pregnant cows an area of farmland can support.

15

2
A NUMBER OF NUMBERS

All over the world, groups of people came up with their own ways of counting and working with numbers. Over time, people made number systems that were easier to use than cuneiform and Egyptian numbers. They were quicker to write, without long confusing strings of symbols.

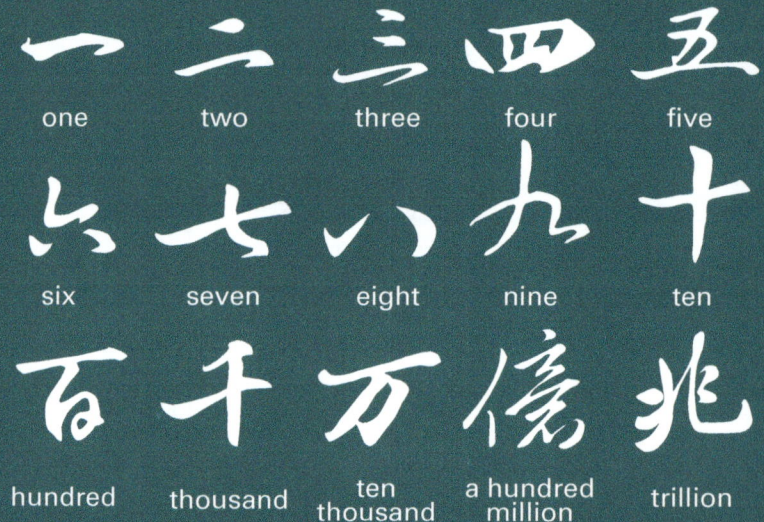

一 one　二 two　三 three　四 four　五 five
六 six　七 seven　八 eight　九 nine　十 ten
百 hundred　千 thousand　万 ten thousand　億 a hundred million　兆 trillion

As some cultures died out and were replaced by others, the way people did math changed.

First in China and later India and the Arab world, mathematicians hit upon using unique symbols for numbers, with a different symbol for each numeral 1–9. They did the same for multiples of 10 and 100. Numbers became shorter, but there were more symbols to learn and remember.

In the end, most of the world settled on the 10 digits we use now, 0-9. It became easier to do calculations—and math got a whole lot easier! Let's see how it happened!

Some cultures still use different numerals.

Roman numerals on clocks are a good example of this.

The Maya of Central America developed numbers independently of Europe and Asia.

 A number of numbers

Write like a Roman

Romans didn't make up symbols to use as numbers. Instead, they used letters to stand for different quantities. It saved learning new squiggles!

I = 1, V = 5, X = 10, L = 50, C = 100, D = 500, M = 1,000

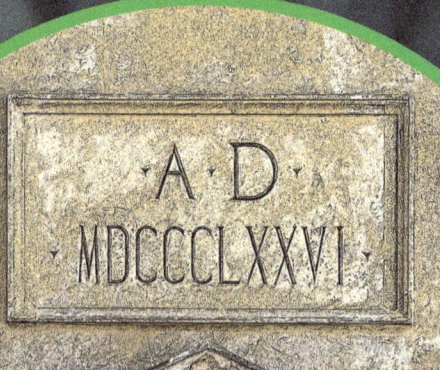

Roman numerals are still sometimes used on buildings—and even for the date in movie credits.

Roman mathematicians had an easier time than those of ancient Egypt and Mesopotamia. Adding symbols for 5, 50, and 500 cut down the repetitions needed. At least a Roman schoolchild never had to write the same letter nine times in a row to make "9"!

The Roman system was mostly additive, meaning you added together the symbols to find the number. Normally, the symbol for the largest number came first, so:

LXXVIII = 50 + 10 + 10 + 5 + 1 + 1 + 1 = 78

The Romans ruled much of Europe for around 500 years, until A.D. 476. Their roads, buildings, and numbers lasted long after they had gone.

There are VIII animals here.

To avoid four identical symbols in a row, Romans moved a smaller number left to show it should be subtracted, so:

IV is 5 (V) – 1 (I) = 4

IX is 10 (X) – 1 (I) = 9

XC is 100 (C) – 10 (X) = 90

Can you figure out what XCIV would be?

It's difficult to do calculations using Roman numerals, but they were used for hundreds of years. People had no choice but to struggle with them!

The split "soroban" abacus is still used in Japan.

TECH TIME

An abacus helped Romans cope with calculations. It's usually a frame with movable beads on wires representing numbers. Each wire can have nine beads, representing 1's, 10's, 100's, and so on, or it can be split with four beads on one side and one on the other. The single bead represents 5 and the four beads stand for 1-4 on each wire.

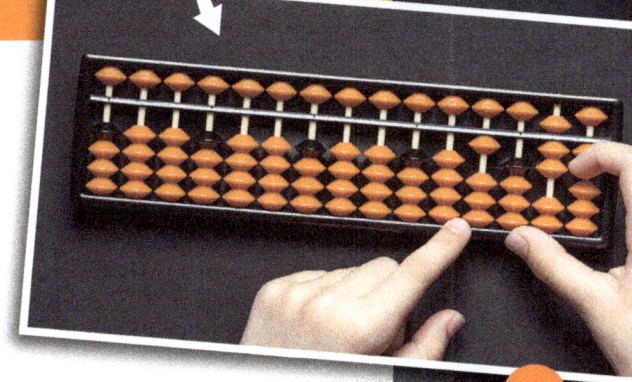

A number of numbers

Chinese numbers

The Chinese system has a separate symbol for each number, 1–10.

Then it adds a new symbol for 100, for 1,000, for 10,000, and so on.

一 二 三 四 五 六 七 八 九 十
1 2 3 4 5 6 7 8 9 10

百　　千　　万
100　1,000　10,000

It uses these with the symbols 1-9 to show how many multiples of 10, 100, 1,000, and so on are needed to make a number, such as 2 × 100 (=200) or 3 × 10 (=30).

To show 12, which is one group of 10 and two groups of 1, first write the 10 and then the 2:

十二

(1 × 10) + (2 × 1) = 12

But to show 20, which is just two groups of 10, the 2 comes first:

二十

(2 × 10) = 20

While people in the West and the Middle East made multiple marks for numbers, people in China had a simpler system. It's sometimes still used, 3,000 years later.

It works the same way with hundreds and thousands. The number 1,985 is written:

一 千 九 百 八 十 五

(1 × 1,000) + (9 × 100) + (8 × 10) + (5 × 1) = 1,985

This is called a multiplicative system, because you have to multiply instead of add to figure out the total.

To show 22, use the 2 twice and the 10 symbol once, for two groups of 10 and two groups of 1:

二 十 二

(2 × 10) + (2 × 1) = 22

The oldest written Chinese numbers are 3,000 years old! They appear on bits of bone and tortoise shell called oracle bones.

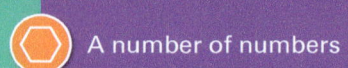
A number of numbers

From India to Baghdad

The Indian Brahmi number system probably began around 2,300 years ago. It had symbols for numbers 1-9 but also special symbols for multiples of ten (20, 30) and of 100 (200, 300).

| 1 | 2 | 3 | 4 | 5 |
| 6 | 7 | 8 | 9 | 0 |

Four camels— but don't write it "4" yet!

0 1 2 3 4 5 6 7 8 9

By around A.D. 600, the numbers had changed. Now, 1, 2, and 3 looked more like their modern versions. But if you could time-travel back 1,400 years, you might be confused if you saw an 8 or a 4 because they were used for our 4 and 5! Eventually, the symbols for 10, 20 and so on disappeared and just the order of the numbers showed their value.

At last we get to modern numbers! The digits 0–9 that are widely used now are called Hindu-Arabic numerals.

01234 56789

These digits could show any number just by the order in which they were written down—it was revolutionary! The Indian mathematician Brahmagupta explained in A.D. 628 how to carry out calculations using them. His work eventually turned up in Baghdad (in what is now Iraq) where Arab scholars were translating and building on ancient knowledge from many cultures. They were on the path to becoming the modern Hindu-Arabic numbers…

Arab and Persian scholars translated important ancient works of science and mathematics into Arabic.

The Persian mathematician **al-Khwarizmi** wrote about the Hindu numerals in the 800's and encouraged people to use them. He made important discoveries including the basic principles of algebra and how to solve equations. The word algorithm (a set of mathematical instructions) comes from his name.

 A number of numbers

New numbers
for a new age

Spain was an Arab land 1,000 years ago. In the 900's, Arabs in Spain started to use the new numbers, but it took another 300 years for more of Europe to catch up.

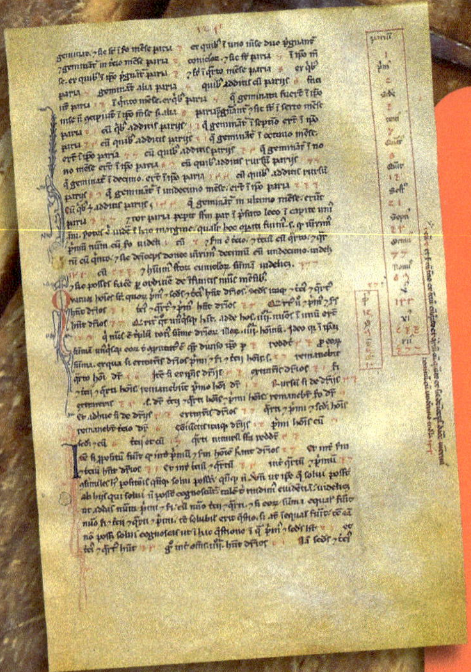

The Italian mathematician Leonardo Fibonacci published a book in 1202 in which he described the new style of numbers he had learned to use on a trip to Algeria in North Africa. He wrote:

"With these nine figures and the sign 0 … any number whatsoever is written."

Fibonacci showed how the new numbers were much better. Not only could he write any number with only nine characters, but calculations were much easier than in any other system.

While the Arab world whizzed ahead in math with their easy-to-use new numbers, Europe was still using Roman numerals—and did so for hundreds of years.

Banking and the start of modern finance began in Italy, and the Italians keenly took to the new numbers. Other parts of Europe were slow to change, some taking until the late 1500's.

With the invention of the printing press in Europe around 1440, the numbers became fixed in their current shapes. They are not likely to change now!

Maybe if the engineers had had better numbers and math, the Leaning Tower of Pisa would have stayed straight!

DID YOU KNOW?

In 1299, the Italian city-state of Florence banned the use of Hindu-Arabic numbers in accounts. People had to use Roman numerals or write the numbers out in full. Some people considered the numbers evil and dangerous because they were not of Christian origin.

Florence, the home of Fibonacci, was at the heart of early Italian banking and finance.

3
GET IN POSITION

We can write even very large numbers using only ten symbols (0-9) because the position of each number tells us what it means. This is called a place-value system, or a positional system, because the place (position) of a numeral shows its value.

Millions	Hundred thousands	Ten thousands	Thousands	Hundreds	Tens	Ones
7	1	5	9	3	6	2

In early number systems, people had to write out long strings of symbols to make numbers. The modern numerals 1-9 make numbers much shorter to write.

Weighing, counting, dealing with money—trading is all about numbers.

India got in first with a full place-value system based on multiples of 10. It was probably first used around A.D. 600. The Sumerian system, used 4,000 years ago, was also a place-value system, but without different symbols for each number up to 9.

Periods	Places	Number of Digits
Crores	Ten Crores (TC) 10,00,00,000	9
Crores	Crores (C) 1,00,00,000	8
Lakhs	Ten Lakhs (TL) 10,00,000	7
Lakhs	Lakhs (L) 1,00,000	6
Thousands	Ten Thousands (T-TH) 10,000	5
Thousands	Thousands (TH) 1,000	4
Ones	Hundreds (H) 100	3
Ones	Tens (T) 10	2
Ones	Ones 1	1

V, IV, III, II, I...
5, 4, 3, 2, 1...

Lots of uses of numbers are possible with a place-value system, and calculations are a whole lot easier now than they were for earlier cultures!

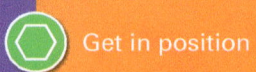 Get in position

Put in your place!

The "2" of "253" shows you it's the largest number, and because it has two more digits after it, you know it represents hundreds. We can do this even with really large numbers:

83,451,325 = 80,000,000 + 3,000,000 + 400,000 + 50,000 + 1,000 + 300 + 20 + 5

The positions relate to powers of 10—that's 1, 10, 100, 1,000, and so on. These are numbers made by multiplying 10 by itself: so 10 × 10 = 100, and 10 × 10 × 10 = 1,000. We add an extra "0" to the end for each multiple of 10 (each power of 10).

Powers of 10	10^1	0^2	10^3	10^4	10^5	10^6
	10	100	1,000	10,000	100,000	1,000,000

Base ten blocks are color-coded to make working in powers of 10 easy: each tiny block is 1, each rod is 10, each square is 100 (10 × 10) and each cube is 1,000 (10 × 10 × 10).

With a place-value system, we could even write the number of sand grains on a beach!

28

A number like 253 can be broken down into 200 + 50 + 3. The positions of the numbers show you their value.

Hundred	Tens	Ones
2	5	3

Hundred	Tens	Ones
2	0	0

The Chinese number system had a special symbol for 100 or 1,000, but a true place-value system relies only on the position of the number to show its value: 200 is two hundred because the 0's in the last two positions show the value of the 2.

Millions (10^6)	Hundred thousands (10^5)	Ten thousands (10^4)	Thousands (10^3)	Hundreds (10^2)	Tens (10^1)	Ones
2	0	3	7	4	8	9

Two million, thirty-seven thousand, four hundred and eighty-nine

Having only one digit for each power of 10 makes it much easier to do calculations. We can use column methods to add and subtract because the position of a number tells us its value. At last people could easily do calculations without needing an abacus!

Even today, herders and shepherds in the Andes use quipu to record their flocks.

TECH TIME

The Inca people in South America used a quipu made of knotted strings to do sums. Each string hanging from a horizontal bar or thread had knots of different styles tied in different positions—or no knot, to show zero. The positions of the knots show their value, up to 10,000.

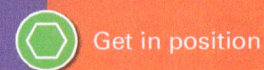
Get in position

Zero, the hero

We use zero (0) to show when there is no value in a position. It's such an important idea that lots cultures around the world came up with their own version of zero independently. The Maya in Central America used a zero, and they had no contact at all with the western world!

In our number system, 103 is made of one 100 and three 1's.

Hundred	Tens	Ones
1	0	3

But if we just wrote 1 3, it would look the same as 13. We use zero to show there are no tens in this number: 103.

The Maya were skilled mathematicians. They developed a calendar that could calculate in thousands of years.

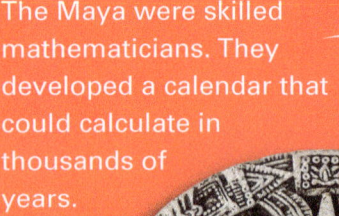

0	1	2	3	4
5	6	7	8	9
10	11	12	13	14
15	16	17	18	19
20	21	22	30	31

DID YOU KNOW?

Numbers never end! You can go on counting forever. Mathematicians talk about infinity as the highest possible number, but there is no highest possible as you can always add one more. So infinity can never be reached. The mathematical symbol for infinity is like an 8 lying down: ∞.

With a place-value system, people only need to learn a small number of symbols and can make very large numbers from them.

But you need to show if there is no number in a particular place.

The idea of no value is so important that early number systems without a zero used a gap or dot to mark an empty place. In the cuneiform system, each position could hold a number up to 60, made from the symbols for 1 and 10.

Sumerian Cuneiform Numerals

1 2 3 4 5
6 7 8 9 10

 **means 3,601:**

60 × 60	60	1
▼		▼

(1 × 60 × 60) + (0 × 60) + (1 × 1)

The space marks an empty place.

But Sumerian math didn't allow a space at the end of number.

 **can mean 61:**

60 × 60	60	1
	▼	▼

(1 × 60) + (1 × 1)

Which number is it?

 **or 3,660:**

60 × 60	60	1
▼	▼	

(1 × 60 × 60) + (1 × 60) + (0 × 1)

The Chinese number system uses ling (零) for zero.

This number means one hundred, no tens, and one unit—101.

一 百 零 一

(1 × 100) + 0 + 1

But ling can only be used once: 1,001 still only has one zero-character! Luckily, we can use as many zeroes as we need, making it easy to write numbers like 1,000,001.

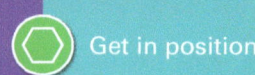
Get in position

Less than zero

With zero, we can count both positive and negative numbers. We count below zero, in negative (minus) numbers, just as we count above zero in positive numbers. Counting things that aren't there might not sound very useful, but it really is!

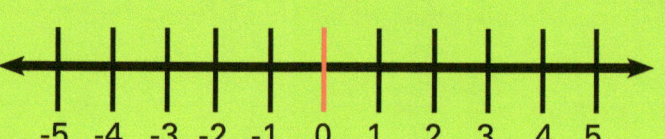

Negative numbers made mathematicians nervous long ago. The ancient Greeks thought them ridiculous: how could you have less than nothing? Their math was based around geometry, working with lines and shapes. These can't have negative length, area, or volume.

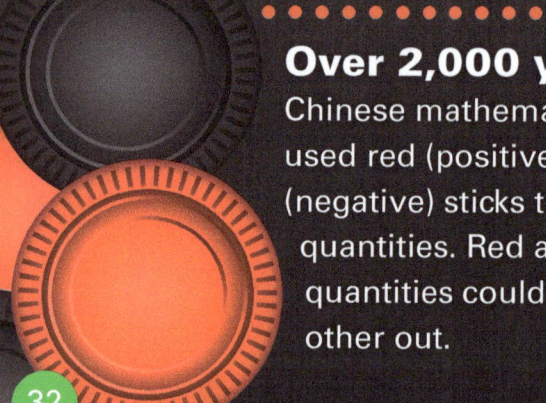

Over 2,000 years ago, Chinese mathematicians used red (positive) and black (negative) sticks to represent quantities. Red and black quantities could cancel each other out.

Negative numbers in an elevator refer to floors below ground level.

Zero is more than just a placeholder showing where there is no value. As the Indian mathematicians first discovered, it's also really useful as a number.

Around A.D. 620, the Indian mathematician Brahmagupta showed how calculations with positive and negative numbers work.

Zero	−	Positive	=	Negative
Zero	−	Negative	=	Positive
Positive	x	Positive	=	Positive
Negative	x	Negative	=	Positive
Positive	x	Negative	=	Negative

Using a number line, it's easy to see that if you subtract 5 from 2, you get −3. If it was 2 °F and the temperature dropped 5 degrees, it would then be -3 °F—very cold!

One common use of negative numbers is in dealing with money. Imagine you have $10, but want to buy something for $15. You borrow $5. Once you have spent the $15, you have −$5, because you will have to pay back the loan:
$10 - $15 = -$5

When you pay back the loan you have:
-$5 + $5 = $0

CURIOUS CONNECTIONS

ASTRONOMY

Astronomers measure the brightness (magnitude) of stars, giving dimmer stars a higher number. The dimmest stars you can see without a telescope are magnitude 6. The brightest object in the sky is the sun, which has a negative magnitude: -26.7. A bright full moon is about -12.

NUMBER BASES

We use base 10 now, too. We use different symbols for each digit up to 9 and then start reusing them. So 1 follows 9 because it has 1 in the 10's column and 0 in the 1's column. If we add another 1, we get 11, which is 1 in the 10's column, and also 1 in the 1's column.

Written	10's	1's
9		9
10	1	0
11	1	1

You could think of the 1s column being full when you've got to 9; if you add another number, it has to spill over into the 10's column and the 1's column empties to start again.

Many historical systems, including the Egyptian, the Roman and the Chinese, introduced new symbols at 10, 100, and 1,000. These are called base 10 systems because they work on powers of 10: 1, 10, 100, 1,000, and so on.

Humans probably use base 10 because we have 10 fingers (including thumbs). If octopuses count, they might use base 8. An octopus would then count like this:

1, 2, 3, 4, 5, 6, 7, 10, 11, 12, 13, 14, 15, 16, 17, 20

(Our equivalent for these numbers is 1, 2, 3, 4, 5, 6, 7, 8, 9, 10, 11, 12, 13, 14, 15, 16.)

The octopus doesn't use the digit 8, just as we don't have a digit for our 10. For the octopus, 8 is 10—1 in the 8's column and 0 in the 1's column. Once the octopus gets to 7, its numbers spill over into the 8's column!

Nine? What's nine? I call that 11!

Using a base 10 abacus, numbers spill over onto the next wire when you get to ten.

Count on your fingers

The Maya in Central America and the Iñupiat of Alaska both used a system based on 5 and 20. Because we have five fingers on each hand, and 20 fingers and toes, it's easy to see how this came about.

Both groups used different symbols for each number up to 19 and then began to reuse symbols for higher numbers. The patterns for building numbers changed at 5, 10, and 15.

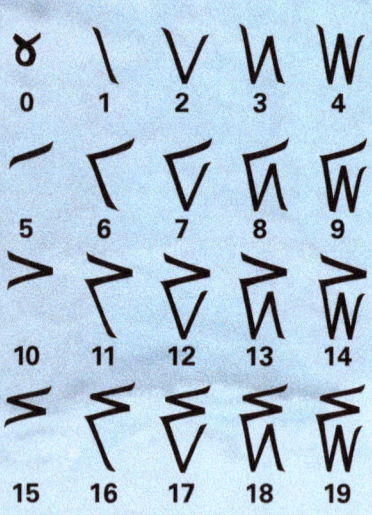

Katkovik numerals of the Iñupiat

Maya numerals

CAREER CORNER

Anthropologists study people and their cultures. Many of the groups that have different counting methods live in remote places, and their ways of life are threatened. Anthropologists collect information about how they live to help preserve their culture and defend their rights.

Humans haven't always used a base 10 system. In the past, and in different parts of the world, other numbers were favored.

Some cultures have used more than just fingers and toes for counting! Several groups in Papua New Guinea, West Papua, Torres Strait Islands, and south-east Australia made counting methods that went around the body. They indicated different body parts for different numbers.

Sumerians counted to 60 on their fingers using three sections of each of four fingers on one hand. They registered each full group of twelve with one of the digits on the other hand—and 5 × 12 = 60.

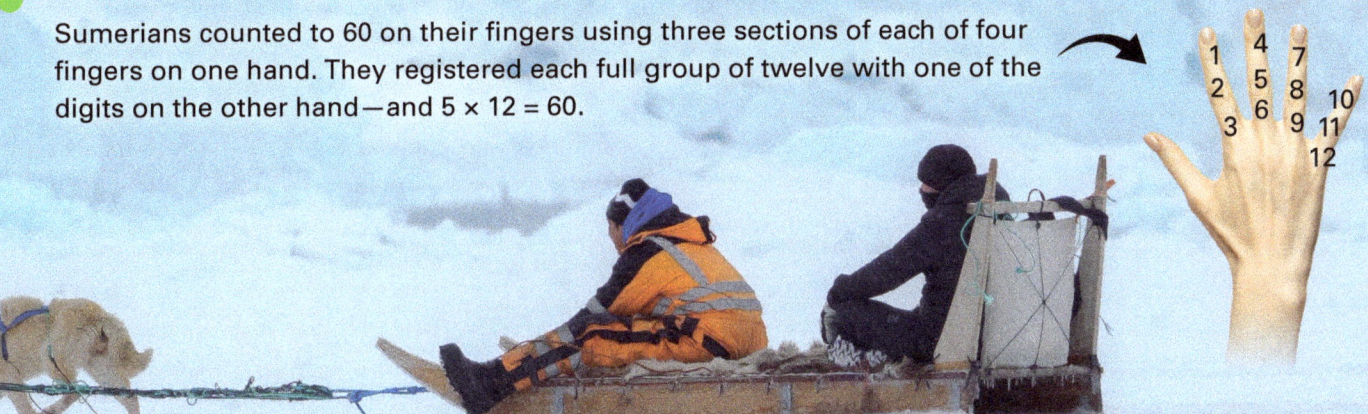

Usually, 1–5 were counted on one hand, then more numbers moved up the arm. They vary after that. The Oksapmin people of Papua New Guinea have a 27-number system that uses body counting starting at one thumb and going over the head to the little finger on the other hand!

Number bases

Dozens of eggs?

The decimal system of measurements used in science is based on 10. One hundred centimeters make a meter and 1,000 meters make a kilometer. But imperial units start again at different numbers. There are 12 inches in a foot, and three feet in a yard. There are 16 ounces in a pound, and eight pints in a gallon.

Computers count in base 2, called binary. Binary has only two digits, 1 and 0. That means that as soon as you get to 2, you write "10" and start again.

1	2	3	4	5	6	7	8	9	10
1	10	11	100	101	110	111	1000	1001	1010

Binary numbers get long very quickly: 99 is 1100011 in binary!

Americans have been using gallons since the first European settlers arrived. They brought the **gallon measure** with them, but there were three different gallons originally. All had the same name, but were different quantities—confusing! The gallon we use now was the wine gallon (231 cubic inches) but there was also a beer gallon (282 cubic inches) and a corn gallon (269 cubic inches).

Although we use base 10 for counting, you come across other bases in everyday life. Lots of American units of measure don't use base 10!

We often count eggs in dozens (12's), and we divide the day into two sets of 12 hours—a.m. and p.m.

Twelve to share?

Twelve is a useful number because it has lots of factors (numbers it can be divided by). Half, a quarter, or a third of 12 is a whole number, which is useful. It's easy to share out 12 cakes between two, three, or four children, or split 12 students into groups to travel on a trip. Ten doesn't have lots of factors. You can divide it in half, but a quarter or a third of 10 is not a whole number. Three children couldn't share 10 cakes evenly without cutting them!

39

 Number bases

60 minutes in an hour

The Sumerian and Babylonian system repeated one symbol for numbers up to 10 and then another in a new position for tens up to 59. This 60-based number system is called sexagesimal. It was super-useful, as 60 has lots of factors: 1, 2, 3, 4, 5, 6, 10, 12, 15, 30, and 60.

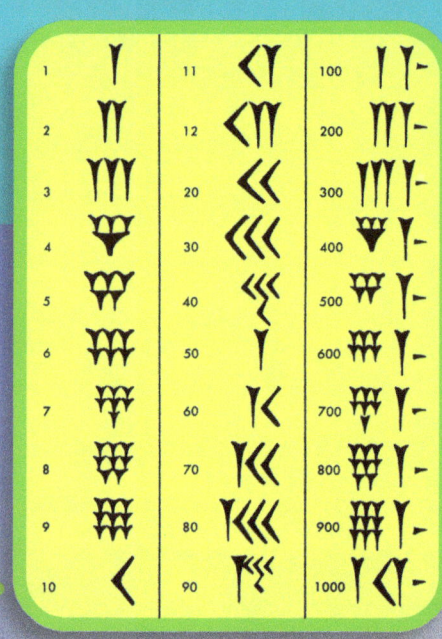

The base 60 system is thousands of years old. There are still bits of it in our lives. Our clocks are based on 60, with 60 seconds in a minute and 60 minutes in an hour. And we divide a circle into 360 degrees. Babylonians didn't have clocks, but they did have circles!

Need to convert time? In the base 60 system, it's as simple as multiplying by 60. The ratio table below demonstrates how 3 hours can be converted into minutes and seconds.

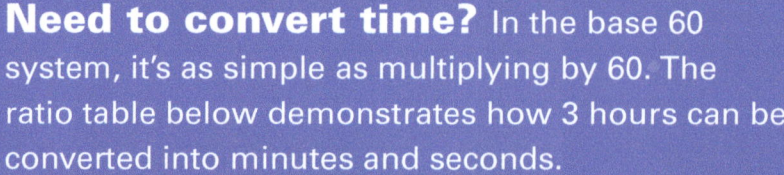

Hours	Minutes	Seconds
3	180	10,800

× 60   × 60

When you count 60 seconds in a minute, you're continuing something started by the Sumerians 4,000 years ago!

A circle is divided into 360 degrees, and each degree can be subdivided into 60 minutes. Those can be further divided into 60 seconds.

Since ancient time, astronomers have used degrees to measure the positions of stars and planets in the sky. Navigators use the points of the compass and a number of degrees to say where something is, or to plot a course.

The world clock in Berlin, Germany, shows the time in 148 major cities of the world in all 24 time zones. Each time zone has 15 degrees of the full circle.

CURIOUS CONNECTIONS

PHYSICS Measuring angles is key to lots of work in astronomy. Astronomers observing a solar eclipse in 1919 worked out from the angle at which starlight is bent when coming around the sun that Einstein's theory of general relativity is correct.

Number bases

Alien numbers

What if an alien species had 13 tentacles or 16 toes? They might use a number system with base 13 or base 16. For aliens with 16 toes, 10 would mean the number we write as 16; it would have 1 in the place for 16's and 0 in the place for 1's. To use their number system, we would have to invent or use different symbols the numbers we write as 10–15.

In fact, lots of computer work uses in base 16, which is called hexadecimal. At their most basic level, computers work with binary (base 2), but numbers are really long in binary. Hexadecimal is easier to read and makes large numbers shorter. Numbers up to 255 need just two digits in hexadecimal.

| 65,536 (= 16 × 16 × 16 × 16) | 4,096 (= 16 × 16 × 16) | 256 (= 16 × 16) | 16 | 1 |

Early computers used paper tape punched with holes to show data in binary, with hole/no hole representing 0 and 1.

Planets beyond our solar system might host life forms with different math systems!

We have no idea if there are intelligent aliens living elsewhere in space, but if there are, they will use some kind of math. It might not be base 10.

Computer programmers use letters for the extra numerals needed: 10 is shown by A, 11 by B, and so on up to F for 15. The number we write as 16 is shown as 10 (1 × 16 + 0 × 1):

1	2	3	4	5	6	7	8	9	10	11	12	13	14	15	16
1	2	3	4	5	6	7	8	9	A	B	C	D	E	F	10
17	18	19	20	21	22	23	24	25	26	27	28	29	30	31	32
11	12	13	14	15	16	17	18	19	1A	1B	1C	1D	1E	1F	20

It gives some funny looking numbers. The number we write as 25 becomes 19 in base 16 (1 × 16 + 9 × 1) and 30 in base 10 becomes 1E (1 × 16 + 14 × 1).

CAREER CORNER

Astronomers use radio telescopes to look for possible signals from intelligent aliens. They can't assume aliens would use base 10 numbers, though. They have to be open to interpreting numbers in any base. When we send information to space, we use binary (base 2) because any intelligent being would recognize it.

Make your own number system!

You will need:
- Paper
- Pencil
- Imagination

Remember, base 5 only goes up to 4, then the numbers spill over to the next column, groups of 5, so we write it as 10—one group of 5 and 0 in the 1's column.

Give it a try

Imagine you are a three-toed sloth, or a spider, or even a millipede or an alien! You are going to devise a counting system based on the number of legs, toes, or some other body part you have. Will you use a place-value system or will you build up numbers from a limited set of symbols, like the Roman system?

1. Invent new symbols for the numbers you need. Draw up a table to show how your new numbers relate to the familiar base 10 numbers:

1	2	3	4	5	6	7	8	9	10	11	...

2. Draw a number line for your new number system. Here's an example of a number line for base 5 as an example

0 1 2 3 4 10 11 12 13 14 20 21

As we have seen, number systems can use any number as a base from 2 to at least 60. Think about what life—and math—would be like using a base other than 10.

3. Find a friend or family member to try out your new number system. You could give them three numbers to translate from base 10 to your number system, and three to translate from your system to base 10.
4. Make up some simple sums in your number system and ask your helper to solve them. Don't make the sums too hard because this is tricky!
5. Convert the numbers back to base 10. Is the answer the same as if you do the sums in base 10? What do you think this tells you about math?

Try this next!

Try creating a system for representing fractions or decimals in your base. How would you show half of something, or 1.5, in your number system?

QUESTION TIME!

How does your new number system make simple calculations like addition and subtraction easier or harder than in base 10?

Index

A
abacuses, 19, 35
algebra, 23
Andes mountains, 29
anthropology, 37
Arabic numbers. *See* Hindu-Arabic numbers
area, 32
astronomy, 13, 33, 41, 43

B
Babylonians, 12, 40
Baghdad, 23
base 10 system, 34-35, 38, 43
base 16 system, 42-43
base 60 system, 40-41
binary numbers, 39-41
Brahmagupta, 23, 33
Brahmi number system, 22
bullas, 11

C
carats, 15
Chinese numbers, 16, 20-21, 29, 31-32, 34
clay, 10-13
click-counters, 9
computers, 39, 42-43
cubits, 14
cuneiform, 12-13, 30

D
daktylos (unit of measure), 15
decimal system, 38
degrees of a circle, 40-41
digits, 17, 23, 27-29, 34-35, 39, 42

E
Egypt, ancient, 13, 15, 34
English tax system, 9
equations, 23
Eswatini, 8

F
Fibonacci, 24-25
Florence, 25

G
gallons, 38-39
Garn (unit of measure), 15
geometry, 32
gourds, 14
Great Sphinx, 13
Greece, ancient, 15, 32

H
Hindu-Arabic numbers, 22-25

I
imperial units, 38
Inca, 29
infinity, 31
Italy, 24-25

K
Khwarizmi, al-, 23

L
Leaning Tower of Pisa, 25

M
Maya, 17, 30, 36
Mesopotamia, 12
multiplicative systems, 21

N
negative numbers, 32-33

O
Oksapmin people, 37
oracle bones, 21

P
physics, 41
Pirahã people, 7
place-value systems, 26-31
printing press, 25
pyramids, 15

Q
quipus, 29

R
radio telescopes, 43
Roman numerals, 17-19, 25, 34

S
Scoville Heat Units (SHU), 15
Spain, 24
spheres, 10
standardization, 14
stars, brightness of, 33
styluses, 13
Sumerians, 12, 27, 30-31, 37, 40-41

T
tallying, 6, 8-9, 11-12
taxes, 9, 13
temperature, 33
time, measurement of, 40-41

V
volume, 14, 32

Z
zero, 29-33

Glossary

algebra (AL juh bruh)—math that uses letters and symbols to show and figure out calculations

area (AIR ee uh)—a measure for the space occupied in two dimensions (length and width) by an object

arithmetic (uh RIHTH muh tihk)—using numbers in calculations such as adding, subtracting, multiplying, and dividing

astronomy (uh STRON uh mee)—the scientific study of space and objects in space, such as stars and planets

carat (KAR uht)—a measure of weight used for precious metals and gems

cuneiform (kyoo NEE uh fawrm)—a form of writing developed in the culture of ancient Sumer, consisting of lines pressed into clay with a wedge-shaped stick called a stylus

digit (DIHJ iht)—the symbol for a single number, such as 5 or 8

equation (ih KWAY zhuhn)—an expression in math that has two equivalent statements separated by an equals sign (=), such as 3 × 7 = 21

gourd (gawrd)—the fruit of a squash plant, or its hollowed, hard outside

hieroglyphs (HY uhr uh glihfs)—picturelike symbols that made up written language in ancient Egypt

Hindu-Arabic numbers—the number symbols we use now, from 0-9

Inca (IHNG kuh)—South American culture that flourished in Peru before the Spanish invasion in the 1500's

Maya (MAH yah)—people who lived in Central America before their culture was destroyed by Spanish invaders in the 1600s

multiplicative (MUHL tuh pli kuh tuhv)—a system of making numbers that works by multiplying numbers together. For example, 23 is made up of 2 × 10 and 3 × 1.

sphere (sfihr)—three-dimensional shape that is circular in cross-section, like a ball

standardized (STAN duhr dyzd)—the same wherever it is used, because it is based on a recognized standard

Sumerian (soo MIHR ee uhn)—belonging to the culture of the city of Sumer, in Mesopotamia

tallying (TAL ee ing)—making a mark corresponding to each of a series of objects of events to keep track of the quantity without counting

tax (taks)—money collected from citizens by a government or state to pay for things that benefit the whole of society, or are needed to run society

volume (VOL yuhm)—a measure of the space occupied in three dimensions (height, width, length) by an object

www.ingramcontent.com/pod-product-compliance
Lightning Source LLC
Chambersburg PA
CBHW061249170426
43191CB00041B/2405